# THE HISTORY OF TATTOOS AND BODY MODIFICATION

Nicholas Faulkner and Diane Bailey

Rosen
YA

Published in 2019 by The Rosen Publishing Group, Inc.
29 East 21st Street, New York, NY 10010

First Edition

**Library of Congress Cataloging-in-Publication Data**

Names: Faulkner, Nicholas, author. | Bailey, Diane, 1966– author.
Title: The history of tattoos and body modification / Nicholas Faulkner and Diane Bailey.
Description: New York : Rosen Publishing, 2019. | Series: Body arts : the history of tattooing and body modification | Includes bibliographical references and index. | Audience: Grades 9–12.
Identifiers: LCCN 2017060224| ISBN 9781508180760 (library bound) | ISBN 9781508180777 (pbk.)
Subjects: LCSH: Tattooing—Juvenile literature. | Body marking—Juvenile literature.
Classification: LCC GN419.3 .F38 2019 | DDC 391.6/5—dc23
LC record available at https://lccn.loc.gov/2017060224

*Manufactured in the United States of America*

# CONTENTS

# INTRODUCTION

Today, we see tattooing, and even body piercings, as commonplace. Walking down the street, any number of people will have one or more of these adornments. While it may seem like a new trend, tattooing is actually rooted in thousands of years of history and tradition. In fact, it is one of the oldest art forms. Archaeologists have even discovered mummies and ancient art that prove people have been getting tattoos for millennia. The earliest tattoos were just simple dots and lines. And the earliest tools used for tattooing were pieces of bone and dyes that were made from plants. The "tattoo parlor" might have been a cave with some good firelight and two people: the artist and the "canvas."

Tattooing is not only an ancient practice; it's a universal one. It is found across all cultures around the world. And while different peoples may display their tattoos for different reasons, they all do it to connect in some way with their communities and the world.

For the ancient Greeks and Romans, tattoos bore mystical powers. Certain groups in China used tattoos to indicate social status, or to which tribe a person belonged. In New Zealand, the Maori tattooed their

Many of today's tattoos have deep roots in history and cultures around the world. The intricate detail of Polynesian tattoos have found their way into Western designs.

entire faces, the design of which indicated status, family history, or the individual's specific skills.

Today's tattoo artists often work to duplicate the delicate details of ancient kanji characters, a type of Japanese writing that actually came from the Chinese. A kanji character uses several small lines that combine to suggest different actions or objects.

In China and Japan, the dragon is an ever-present tattoo. Dragons are powerful—but good—creatures. They're intelligent, wise, and brave. Plus, they bring good luck and wealth. Chinese dragons are varied: the celestial dragon takes care of heaven, while the Earth dragon is in charge of Earth. The horned dragon is strong, while the hornless yellow dragon is celebrated for its knowledge. In Japan, a dragon's coloring indicates its personality and traits. Green dragons represent life and the earth. Black dragons have the advantage of experienced, wise parents. As tattoos, dragons offer a wide array of meanings and a host of artistic possibilities.

In many tribes around the world, the more tattoos a person has, the more important he or she is. The most powerful and influential individuals are often those who have proven their skill in hunting, or by fighting enemies. These actions are traditionally recognized—and rewarded—by receiving a tattoo.

Tattooing in the Western world has developed its own style over the centuries. However, as with all art, it was influenced by other cultures over time. Over thousands of years, tattoo art evolved on the islands of Polynesia, in the jungles of South America, and on the plains of North America. When Europeans came into contact with these cultures, tattoos changed. Over the next two hundred years, the free-thinking, progressive attitudes of Western people had a huge influence on tattoo art. People from Europe and the United States introduced new designs and styles of art. They also introduced new reasons for getting tattoos.

The next time you see someone wearing a tattoo, understand that they are practicing an ancient art form. The design, though unique, may have evolved over hundreds or thousands of years of history and tradition.

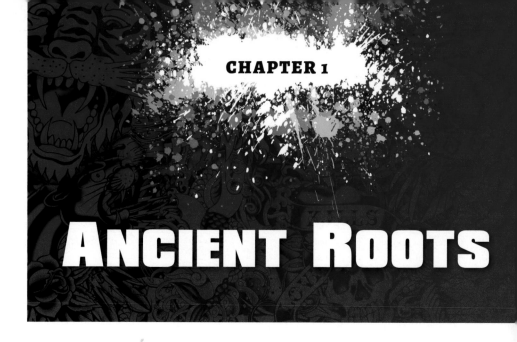

# CHAPTER 1

# ANCIENT ROOTS

n 1991, hikers in the Alps made an incredible find. On the border of Italy and Austria, under a few layers of snow and ice, they found the preserved corpse of a man. When archaeologists studied the man, they determined he was old—more than five thousand years old! But instead of his body having rotted away, leaving only the bones, this man was remarkably intact. He had been preserved by the freezing temperatures. He was named Ötzi after the Ötztal Alps where he was discovered.

Because his skin had not decayed, scientists found many tattoos on Ötzi's body—more than fifty altogether. Small dots and lines had been placed on his lower spine, behind his knee, and on his ankle. Researchers pointed out that these areas corresponded to acupuncture points. Acupuncture is a traditional type of Chinese medicine. Needles are inserted into the skin at certain places to help relieve pain or other ailments. Scientists

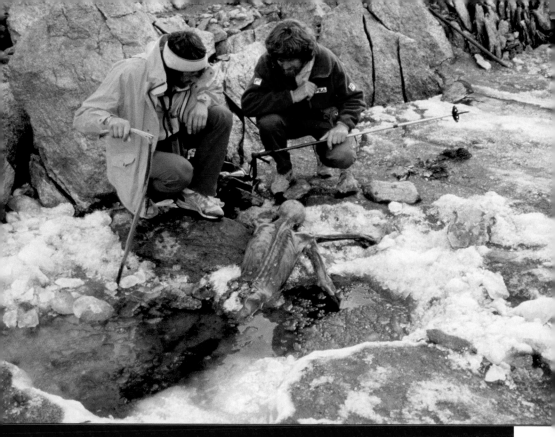

In September 1991, two mountaineers discovered the mummified remains of a man whom scientists named Ötzi. Though he was thousands of years old, his tattoos were still visible.

believed Ötzi's tattoos might have been for the same reason. Also, his tattoos would have normally been covered up by his clothes, so they probably weren't there to be decorative.

Tattooed mummies from about 2,400 years ago have also been found in Siberia, a remote part of Russia. These mummies were part of a tribe of people called the Pazyryks. One of the bodies was covered in elaborate animal tattoos, including a donkey, a fish, rams, and deer. This mummy was probably the body of the tribe's chief. The tattoos were a way to show how important he was within the tribe. There were other pictures of mythical animals like griffins. Scientists think that the Pazyryks believed these fantastical creatures had magical properties which would protect or strengthen the person who wore them. Like Ötzi, the chief also had several small circles tattooed along his spine and on his ankle, probably to help with sickness or injuries.

The Picts were a people who lived from about 7,000 BCE to 850 CE in the area that is now Scotland. The Romans described them with the Latin word "Pictii," which means "the painted ones." According to reports, they had pictures of birds, fish, and other animals tattooed all over their bodies. The Picts used iron needles to prick the skin.

Although these are the earliest people found with tattoos, archaeologists have found tattoo needles and pigments that date from the Upper Paleolithic period (38,000 BCE to 10,000 BCE). Tattooing may have been going on for longer than we know.

The earliest tattoo designs were abstract patterns, but these eventually turned into pictures. Among the first evidence of a pictorial tattoo was in the form of the ancient Egyptian god Bes. Bes was a household god. He was there when babies were born. He protected objects that came into contact with people, such as chairs or dishes. He was also in charge of fun. Music, dancing, and general partying all came under Bes's command. Images of Bes have been found tattooed on female Nubian mummies from about 400 BCE, and can be seen on the thighs of musicians and dancers in paintings from ancient Egypt.

## BODY ART IN EGYPT, ROME, AND GREECE

In ancient Egypt, it seems that only women received tattoos. Mummies from four thousand years ago revealed women with elaborate patterns of dots and

Tattoos are evident on the mummified remains of this Scythian warrior. The Scythians were Eurasian nomads who flourished from about the ninth to the first centuries BCE.

dashes. The tattoos were probably related to fertility. They were believed to help a woman to have children.

Ancient Greeks and Romans also wore tattoos. The Greeks adopted the practice from the Persians, who were their neighbors. In turn, the Greeks passed it on to the Romans. Some of the most famous wars ever happened among these cultures. The Greeks and the Persians fought it out for fifty years during the Greco-Persian Wars. The Roman empire was extremely powerful, and frequently engaged in military action to make it even more powerful. Soldiers were sometimes tattooed so that if they tried to desert—leave the army without permission—they could easily be recognized.

Ancient tribal cultures considered tattoos to be status symbols. The Greeks and Romans, on the other hand, used tattoos to punish people. A tattoo was a way to, quite literally, make a "black mark" against somebody's character. The Latin word for tattoo meant "stigma." Today, that word refers to something that is shameful and will hurt a person's reputation.

Plato was an influential Greek thinker. He believed that people who were guilty of sacrilege should be tattooed and banned from society. Plato was just reflecting the attitudes of his time, however. He was generally considered to be a reasonable, intelligent man. Not so the Roman emperor Caligula.

# TATTOOING METHODS AND DESIGNS

With the exception of a few mummies found in snow-drifts or Egyptian tombs, there aren't that many surviving bodies from thousands of years ago. Most information about tattoos comes from sources other than actual skin. There are a few written records telling about tattoo practices. Most evidence, however, comes from art. Paintings and statues that have survived through the years show people with tattoos on their bodies.

Although the earliest tattoos used dots and dashes that were easy to draw, these could be combined into elaborate patterns and designs for a striking look. Abstract, geometric patterns might cover large portions of the body.

Prehistoric people often used charcoal, or soot, as a pigment for tattoos. Ötzi's tattoos included a little bit of quartz, which made them glitter. Scientists aren't sure whether this was added on purpose, for a glitzy effect, or whether it just got in by accident.

In ancient Rome, a doctor recorded a recipe for tattoo ink. It included the wood and bark of an acacia tree, as well as corroded bronze mixed with vinegar, gall (bile from an animal), and vitriol (sulfuric acid). The ingredients were combined into a powder, then soaked in water and juice from a leek (which is like a large green onion). The Celts used a plant called woad. The dye that came out of this plant made indigo, which was a deep blue color.

*(continued on the next page)*

Today, tattoos are applied with sophisticated and sterilized tattoo guns. Throughout history, however, many different tools and materials were used to practice the art.

*(continued from the previous page)*

In the Americas, native tribes pricked the skin, and then sometimes rubbed color into the cuts. The Inuit people of the Arctic regions actually "sewed" on tattoos: they coated a thread with pigment, threaded it through a needle, and then used the needle to puncture the skin and pull the thread through. In Polynesia, a small, sharp comb was dipped into pigment, then placed on the skin and tapped (rather violently) to transfer the pigment into the skin.

By all accounts, Caligula was strange. He was also cruel. He knew tattoos would damage a person's reputation, so he had members of his court tattooed.

Historically, tattoos were assigned mystical powers. They protected the wearer from dangerous spirits, and improved his position with the gods. Being tattooed showed a person's importance in a tribe. The specific designs or pictures indicated what his skills were, who his family was, and what kind of person he was. It was believed that a person could channel the spirit of his tattoo. For example, a picture of a tiger could make someone fierce. An eagle gave strength and spiritual power, while a hawk showed self-discipline. A dog, which was traditionally man's best friend, represented loyalty. As tattoos evolved from abstract designs into pictures, animals became the most popular category, and they remain so today.

Centuries ago, people had much less contact with others outside their own cultures. Customs, traditions, and art developed independently of each other. Tribal cultures in the Polynesian Islands, Africa, and the Americas all had tattoos—but they each had their own style.

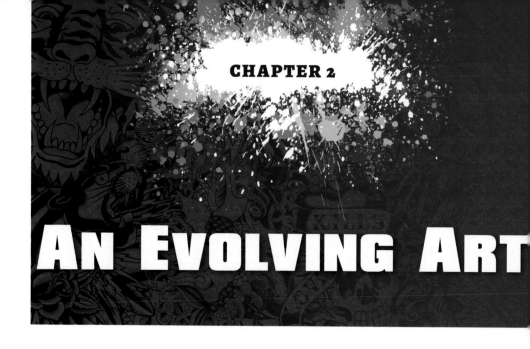

# CHAPTER 2

# AN EVOLVING ART

M any of today's tattooing styles are rooted in the past. With current inking techniques, artists can create the most cutting-edge designs. However, some of the tried-and-true styles continue to be popular.

Like any other type of art, tattooing has developed in different styles. Traditional, or old school, tattooing ruled in the late 1800s and early 1900s. Pictures of anything from butterflies to Betty Boop come under the traditional category. These designs are simple and strong, but not necessarily realistic. New school designs might be modern, exotic, or fantastical. They use a broader array of colors and more blending and shading.

Black and gray, or jailhouse, is a style that started in prisons. Tattoo artists used homemade equipment, and they did not have any colored ink. Instead, they

Tattooing is an ever-evolving art. It mixes the history and traditions of a variety of cultures. Artists today try to push the boundaries of what they can do.

used a makeshift dye made from cigarette ashes. Without color, black and gray tattoos depend on the artist's ability to use line and shading.

Fine line tattooing opened the door to even more designs. These tattoos are detailed, realistic paintings. Instead of a general image of a person, a fine line tattoo can produce a picture of an actual person—like a snapshot on your skin. Because these designs are so intensely detailed, tattooists have to be careful. Unlike the canvas of a painting, the skin gets saggy and wrinkly over time—and so will whatever's on it. Fine line tattoos are especially vulnerable.

Chicano tattooing began in the Southwest, among Latin gangs, about the middle of the twentieth century. Chicano tattoos were done in a black-and-white, fine line style which was ideal for portraits, and often used Catholic imagery, such as pictures of Jesus. Today, Chicano tattoos may also use color, as well. This style of tattooing made possible some of the highly detailed designs we see today.

Biomechanical tattooing started in the late 1970s and early 1980s. These tattoos look a little bit like funky X-rays. The tattoo seems to strip away the skin, revealing the layers underneath. However, instead of just bones and blood vessels, these tattoos show a combination of gears and wires, as well as the living parts of the body.

All of these styles are still in use today. However, as the demand for tattoos grows, so does the desire for more, and different, designs. Customers used to walk into a tattoo parlor and choose from the flash on the wall. Flash was a collection of pictures showing possible tattoos. Many were mass-produced images that were available many places. Today, clients often request a custom design, which may combine different styles and will be unique to the wearer.

## THE ART OF LETTERING AND CALLIGRAPHY

A picture might be worth a thousand words, but sometimes a word is all you need. In addition to patterns and

Tattoo calligraphy is an art all its own. There's an endless variety of fonts and styles artists can use to deliver a message that is personal, meaningful, and beautiful.

pictures, a popular tattoo choice today is with lettering. A simple proclamation of "family" or "pride" clearly states the wearer's priorities. Initials are another approach. These might be of a person's name, or the first letters of the words in a motto. For example, the letters "LYD" — for "Live Your Dreams" —might be artistically intertwined to make a pleasing symbol, as well as a statement.

Old English, Gothic-style lettering has a strong, imposing look and is often chosen by gang members or other people wanting to project a tough image. This

## TRIBAL DESIGNS TODAY

Traditional tribal tattoos are also gaining new ground, not only among the tribes that originated them, but among people in all cultures. New tribalism got its start in the 1990s and had a surge of interest over the next decade. While no longer considered cutting-edge, this style still appeals to many.

Leo Zulueta is a tattooist who is often named as the artist who started the modern tribal movement in Western tattoos. He said, "I think the kind of people that are drawn to [new tribalism] are looking for some kind of deeper thing, something deeper than the high-tech society that we live in."

Part of the return to tribalism, sometimes called modern primitive, has to do with the designs. They are simple yet striking. A deeper reason lies with the experience itself. By turning to an ancient ritual such as tattooing, people feel that they can reconnect with history. They are channeling an activity that gives them access to a community that would otherwise be lost.

According to tattoo artist Lyle Tuttle, for some people, getting a tattoo is "a form of finding their lost tribal ancestry." In some cases, these ancient cultures have been stamped out, but tattoos can provide a link to what once existed. Of course, the tattoo designs may not be exactly the same as they were centuries ago. For example, in the 1960s, American Peace Corps volunteers on Samoa sometimes got an armband tattoo before they left. Anthropologists aren't sure who had this idea first. Was the armband a traditional Samoan tattoo? Or did the volunteers introduce it? Either way, those visitors to the islands brought back tattoos that represented a life that was both simple and exotic.

style of lettering was—and still is—used in prisons, and has come to be associated with criminal activity. However, its bold lines also make it a good choice when combined with other tattoo styles, such as Celtic or tribal designs.

Another distinctive lettering style comes from graffiti art. The fat and funky letters of this street art evoke the creativity and playfulness of hip-hop. The curves of Arabic or Sanskrit (an ancient language from India) can mimic the curves of the body.

Also on the rise is Asian lettering. Many Asian languages do not use an alphabet that combines letters or sounds into words. Instead, these languages use characters that represent an object or even an entire idea. Asian symbols representing "peace," "love," or "harmony" are especially popular in the West.

Tattoo artists who specialize in calligraphy will also work with clients to design their own lettering styles. These can express their own personal style and can be customized to work with other tattoos.

Tattoo calligraphy has endless creative potential to span different cultures and languages. The tattoo can display a meaningful message and be aesthetically pleasing.

## WHEN CULTURES COME TOGETHER

The act of tattooing has gone mainstream. It's a stream that is powered by artistic currents from cultures all over the world. They have blended and mixed with each other. People are combining elements from different societies. It wouldn't be strange to see a man from Germany with an Aztec sun god, a Polynesian man with a race car, or an American soccer mom with a Celtic cross.

Design styles have also started to blend together. The elaborate chest markings of the Marshall Islands might be used in conjunction with the distinctive Tā Moko facial tattooing of New Zealand's Maori. Japanese styles have had a tremendous effect. "The whole world of traditional Japanese art and tattooing is very influential in today's modern tattooing to the point where almost every tattoo reflects a lesson taken from Japanese art," Seattle tattoo artist Damon Conklin said in a *Smithsonian* magazine article. The full-body Japanese tattoo might tell the story of traditional Japanese heroes, or it could be done with Batman and the Joker battling it out on the streets of Gotham.

East and West have traded back and forth so much that they've nearly reversed themselves. In the United States, people love Eastern symbolism, such as Asian characters that represent spiritual enlightenment. In Asia, youths tend to choose flashy, specific images from Western culture.

Over the centuries, tattoos have served many functions. They've been a way to heal the body, prove religious devotion, and show someone's status in society. But now, perhaps no other art form is so intensely individual. Tattoo art is as varied as the artists who design it and people who get it.

Add them up, and the world's people probably have billions of tattoos. But no two are quite the same. They are not simply pictures, but choices. Tattoos are an art form that reaches millions, but remains the most personal of them all.

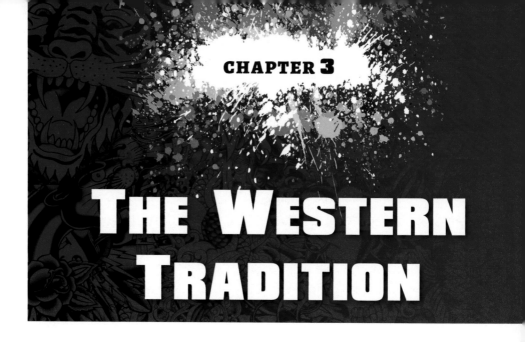

# CHAPTER 3

# THE WESTERN TRADITION

When British explorer James Cook returned from his trip to the South Pacific in 1771, he didn't bring souvenirs home to his family and friends. Instead, he and his crew brought something few people in Britain (or the rest of Europe) had ever seen: a tattoo.

In Britain, tattoos had been fashion no-nos. But sailors liked them, and they started to make a comeback. Rather than copy tribal tattoos, sailors chose symbols that represented the details of their own lives. Tattoos could be both good luck charms (they were hard to lose) as well as symbols that the sailor was part of a fraternity. Anchors were popular, since they represented stability, which was not always possible on a stormy sea. A pig on one foot and a rooster on the other was believed to protect a sailor from drowning, since neither of those animals could swim.

This tattoo is a memorial to those killed in the September 11, 2001, terrorist attacks. Iconic images, such as national flags, are just one type of tattoo style common in the Western tradition.

Western designs used identifiable pictures, as opposed to the abstract patterns that tribal cultures favored. Also, unlike the detailed, full-body tattoos of the Japanese, Western tattoos were smaller and simpler. Instead of having one large tattoo, a person was more likely to have a collection of smaller ones. This came out of the sailor tradition. A sailor might get one tattoo in Singapore and another in Hong Kong. They became mementos of where he had been. One tattoo didn't tell the whole story—as it might in a full-body Japanese tattoo. Instead, it was a picture or symbol that represented the story.

Tattooing spread to other branches of the military, as well. In the United States, especially during wartime, servicemen might prove their loyalty with patriotic images such as flags, eagles, and Uncle Sam—a crusty old guy representing the government. Americana—symbols and designs representing things that were uniquely American—were also popular. It might be a Coca-Cola bottle or a cartoon character like Mickey Mouse. In the 1960s, the biker culture exploded. These motorcyclists traveled in packs and projected a tough image. They flocked to Harley-Davidson motorcycles, and the company's logo started showing up on the arms of motorcycle enthusiasts. Later, other fringe groups—like hippies or punks—took up tattooing.

For much of the twentieth century, tattoo art in the United States was straightforward and relatively simple. However, by the 1970s, this old school style was evolving. Artists began to adopt the rich colors and lavish details of Japanese tattooing, as well as the fantastical images. In the United States, the size and detail of a Japanese tattoo was mixed with American imagery. More than anything, the Western tradition was a soup of ideas, borrowed from all the world's cultures and then combined with the bigness and brashness of Western thought.

## VIKING RUNES AND CELTIC KNOTS

Tattoo art in most of Western Europe mirrors what is seen in the United States. However, some styles draw on Europe's older cultures. The Vikings were a seafaring people who dominated Scandinavia, in Northern Europe, more than a thousand years ago. The Celts are even older. They thrived in Britain, Scotland, Ireland, and other parts of Europe from about 500 BCE to 400 CE. People who can trace their ancestry to these peoples are especially attracted to tattoos that reflect these cultures. Vikings used a form of writing using symbols called runes. Runes are pictorial symbols that tell a story.

Viking runes, such as these engraved on a gravestone, are symbols used to tell a story. Runes found their way into many Viking and Celtic tattoo styles.

They also had power of their own. They could be used to see the future, or cast a spell. As tattoos, runic

# A WAY TO EXPRESS YOURSELF

In Europe and the United States, tattoos became the marks of a new class of outcasts, associated with men who were rough and crude. Sailors were far too rough to be accepted into polite society. Punks, hippies, and bikers belonged to their own groups and were happy to stay there. Like the slaves of ancient Rome, or the criminals of ancient Japan, they were outsiders, but in these cases, they were proud of it.

Today, the motives behind getting a tattoo sometimes seem contradictory. On the one hand, they might

Bikers are one group that uses tattoos to promote inclusion and camaraderie. While many biker groups cast themselves as outsiders, their tattoos identify them as insiders in their own community.

be a way to associate oneself with a particular group. On the other hand, they might be a way to express individuality. The desire to be different can even put the person back into a group—people who want to be different!

Why a person gets tattooed, what design she chooses, what part of her body she gets tattooed—all these factor into the decision to get a tattoo. It might be a fashion statement or a way to remember a loved one or a special time. It might be a symbol of individuality or identity, or an image that proclaims a person's commitment to a group, religion, or philosophy.

While many tribal and Eastern cultures recognized the beauty of tattoos, few of them celebrated tattoos as a way to advertise a person's individuality. Western cultures added that significance to the process of tattooing.

designs are both intricate and simple. For the wearer, they combine visual artistry with deeper power. A *vegvisir* is a kind of compass that provides direction for the wearer. The fylfot is in the shape of a swastika. During World War II, the German Nazi government used the swastika sign and it became associated with tyranny and evil. However, for centuries before, the swastika was a good-luck symbol.

Probably the best-known Celtic design theme is a knot. Lines can be braided together in an intricate pattern or merely crossed once or twice in the ultimate simplicity. Knot tattoos are often encased in circles. These maze-like designs symbolize the connections in life. Crosses and triskeles—a pattern resembling a three-pronged swirl—are other Celtic designs frequently translated into tattoos. Although the imagery of Celtic designs can be similar to tribal tattoos, they were actually adopted from other forms of art.

## TATTOOING AND RELIGION

Historically, the Eastern European countries of Bosnia, Albania, and Croatia—an area known as the Balkans—have formed a fence. On one side was Western Europe, which was mostly Christian. On the other were the countries that practiced Islam. When the Turks invaded the Balkans in the fifteenth century, they brought Islam with them. Many Balkans became Muslim. However, some stayed Christian. These Christians often received a tattoo to signify their religion. For girls, this was usually a cross on their hands, arms, or shoulders. Boys were less likely to get tattooed, although they might receive a small cross on their fingers. Christians might have gotten these tattoos voluntarily. It's also possible the Turks forced them to do it to mark them. Either way, the tradition continued well into the twentieth century, with teenage girls gathering at church on Catholic holidays to receive a tattoo and make this rite of passage.

As Christianity spread throughout Europe, the popularity of tattooing began to fade. Christians believed tattoos were the marks of pagans and heathens, people who did not honor the true God. They pointed to a verse in the Bible that said God prohibited tattooing. Interestingly, tattoos also became a way to show religious devotion. Despite the Biblical warning against it, Christian pilgrims—people who took a long journey to a holy place—often got a tattoo as proof of their visits.

Some people use religious images and iconography, such as this illustration of Jesus Christ, to show their commitment to their faith.

Today, religious tattoos are a growing category. Some Christians show their faith by inking tattoos of crosses, pictures of Jesus, Bible verses, or even more elaborate scenes. A growing number of younger Christians gravitate to the basic ideas of Christianity, but still want the freedom to express themselves. They might use the tattoos to inspire them or reinforce their faith.

Jews are more resistant to the idea. During World War II, Jewish prisoners were tattooed by German Nazis to identify them. Not only was this cruel, but it also violated a Jewish law, to not have the body tattooed. Today, however, the practice of tattooing is gaining some acceptance among Jews, especially younger ones. The horrors of World War II are not as fresh, and the influence of Western popular culture is everywhere. Even traditionally Jewish nations such as Israel are seeing an upswing.

In some parts of the world, Muslims also struggle with the question of whether to get tattoos. Officially, the religion forbids it, but some Muslims reject this point of view and get them anyway.

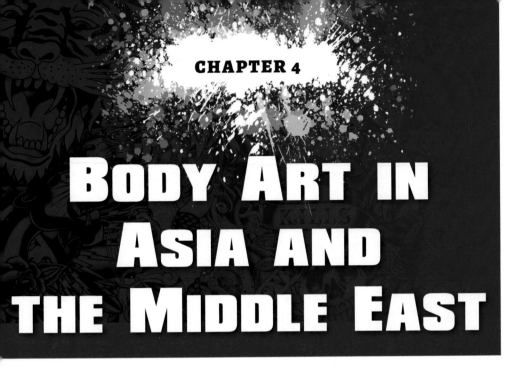

# CHAPTER 4

# BODY ART IN ASIA AND THE MIDDLE EAST

Asian and Middle Eastern tattoo art can be much different from that in the West. However, people across all cultures get tattoos for similar reasons. Sometimes it's simply for artistic beauty. Other times it's for more symbolic purposes, such as religion or remembrance.

## IN CHINA

As with many Asian countries, the traditions of Chinese tattooing are sometimes contradictory. Ethnic groups in China historically used tattoos to show social status. A tattoo would also indicate to which tribe a person belonged. Certain villages were vulnerable to enemy attacks. Sometimes the women would tattoo themselves to make themselves less attractive to the men from these tribes. If they were kidnapped, the tattoos helped identify them to rescue parties.

However, for centuries Chinese society frowned on tattooing. Tattoos were used to punish outcasts and criminals. In the 1960s, China's leader Mao Zedong outlawed tattoos. Even today, they are not widely accepted. Members of the military are not permitted to have tattoos, and many private businesses refuse to hire people with tattoos.

Not surprisingly, traditional tattooing is dying out, although it still hangs on in certain tribes. The Drung people of southwest China tattoo girls at about age twelve or thirteen to show their maturity. Lines are drawn around the mouth, on the cheeks and between the eyebrows to represent a butterfly.

The Dai people have similar customs. Women get tattoos on their hands, arms, and faces to enhance their beauty. Men want to advertise their bravery and strength, so they tattoo the body's muscular parts: backs, chests, and biceps.

To show the Chinese government the importance of preserving these old customs, recently the China Association of Tattoo Artists helped some elderly women from the Dulong tribe leave their village for the first time ever, to show off their tattoos at a convention.

Also, influences from Western cultures are creeping into China. As the country struggles for more individual rights, tattoos are slowly gaining acceptance.

## IN THAILAND

Thai people believe in the magical powers of tattoos. If they survive a brush with death, they often give credit to the protective power of their tattoos. The process of receiving a tattoo is accompanied by special rituals in order to acti-vate its magical powers. Afterward, a person may have to observe certain behaviors in order to keep his tattoo working. The Thai also believe that too many tattoos can interfere with a person's per-sonality, and that some people simply don't have the mental strength to handle certain tattoos.

Tattooing is often a symbol of a rite of passage in many cultures. In some Chinese traditions, women tattoo their faces when they reach maturity.

## TATTOOING IN BUDDHISM

Buddhism is the dominant religion in Thailand today, but this country has a long history of tribal cultures that started in its dense forests. Tattoos often combine these histories. Tattooing is especially popular in rural areas and among the lower classes. However, the Thai government officially opposes tattooing. People who apply for government jobs must show their chests and arms to prove that they have no tattoos. To get around this, some people have their tattoos applied with invisible ink.

*Sak yant*, or *yantra*, tattooing is a religious form of tattooing that is prevalent in Thailand, Laos, and Cambodia. It is also spreading to parts of China. Sak yant symbols represent Buddha's sacred teachings. Pictures of animals, gods, and divine words are part of *sak yant* tattoos. People get them to bring good fortune and luck.

Tattooing is a highly ceremonial process among Buddhist monks. The process is far removed from the sterile tattoo parlor in today's cities. Instead, the monks sometimes get hypnotized before they are tattooed with swords that have been dipped in ink.

## IN BURMA, VIETNAM, AND INDIA

The Shan ethnic group is a tribe originally from Burma (now Myanmar). To show their strength and maturity, Shan men received tattoos stretching from their waists to their knees. Animals and geometric patterns were etched with indigo ink by the tribe's medicine man. Today, Buddhist symbols are popular among the Shan tribe. Soldiers and police might choose a black tiger to protect them from death. A parrot is believed to bring good luck.

However, as in other Asian countries, the Burmese government officially opposes tattoos. At a recent concert, hip-hop star G-Tone pulled up his shirt onstage, showing a tattoo on his back. He was arrested. Also, pictures of tattooed people are not allowed to be printed in newspapers or magazines. The tattoos have to be removed with computer technology.

Traditional tattooing does survive in some isolated regions, such as the high mountains and dense

In remote regions of Burma (now Myanmar), Vietnam, and India, there is also a tradition of women tattooing their faces for various symbolic reasons, such as passage into adulthood or to promote social ranking, among other reasons.

forests of Vietnam and Burma. For example, the Chin province in Burma is home to the Chinbok tribe. They are named for their tradition of women tattooing their chins. Each woman has her own individual design.

In India, people are strictly divided into social classes, or castes. Women's tattoos usually showed that they were inferior to men. Their tattoos also were believed to increase their fertility and make them attractive to men. Men of the upper castes usually got fewer tattoos than men in the lower castes.

## IN JAPAN

Japan's neighbors, the Chinese, observed as early as 300 CE that Japanese men, young and old, were tattooed all over. The Chinese, however, believed tattoos were undesirable. The Japanese eventually came around to this way of thinking. In the eighth century, a Japanese emperor was deciding on the fate of a traitor. Death was the accepted punishment. But perhaps the emperor was in a good mood, because he decided to be merciful. Instead of death, the man was sentenced to tattooing.

This overall attitude persisted for another one thousand years. Tattooing was illegal, reserved as a punishment for criminals and outcasts. Maybe that was better than death—or maybe not. It was not a "slap on the wrist" that was easily forgotten. Instead, people with tattoos were literally marked for life. Their families and friends no longer spoke to them, and they weren't able to join in community life.

A Japanese gang called the Yakuza thought tattoos were the perfect way to show their commitment. The pain of getting a tattoo proved their bravery. The permanence of a tattoo showed that they would be loyal forever. And since tattoos were illegal, it bound them together as outlaws. It was like a membership card that never got lost!

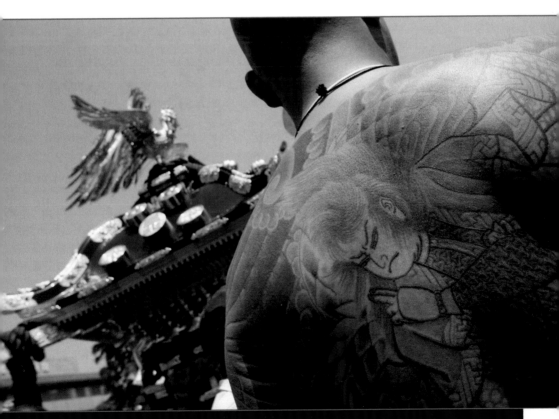

The Yakuza are a Japanese gang that uses tattoos to show their bravery and loyalty to the other members of their group. Tattoos in Japan are often looked down upon and associated with criminal activity.

By the end of the seventeenth century, decorative tattooing was becoming more popular. Even though it was illegal, it was still a flourishing art. The full-body tattoo has its roots in Japan. Traditional Japanese tattoos—called *horimono*—were often single, large designs. They might be of famous heroes, or have religious meanings. They covered a person's back, stretched up his arms and down his legs, and sometimes curled around to his chest. Besides the central figures, Japanese tattoos pay close attention to backgrounds, as well as to the colors and shading of the design.

Tattooing is now legal in Japan, but tattoos are still often seen as symbols of criminal activity. People with tattoos may be shunned in public places like subways. The full-body tattoo has dropped in popularity. Even members of the Yakuza now opt for a simpler design on the arm.

Some younger people are starting to rediscover tattooing, but they are attracted more to Western-style designs than traditional Japanese ones. Tattoos are increasingly popular among women, however, because they are more likely to follow the fashion trends of Western cultures.

## IN THE MIDDLE EAST

Two cultures in the Middle East have had a huge influence on tattooing. The Bedouin are an Arab people (their name means "people who live in the desert.") The Nawar were Gypsies in the region. The Nawar usually tattooed the Bedouin, as well as themselves. This tradition is not as widespread as it once was, but it still exists in places. However, the designs used by Gypsies and Bedouin are different. Although the two cultures share a tradition of tattooing, they remain separate by using distinct tattoo designs.

Tattoos were a way for women to attract men. They often tattooed their chins with an extensive pattern of blue stars. Some women still may

In the Bedouin tradition, women would often tattoo their chins with a pattern of blue stars as a mark of beauty.

get tattoos between their eyebrows, often a triangle of crossed lines.

Islam is the main religion in the Middle East. Its followers are called Muslims. Tattooing is prohibited under Islamic law, and many Middle Eastern governments forbid the practice. However, tattooing has been around longer than Islam in the Middle East. Tribes from Egypt, North Africa, and Asia all helped develop a tattooing tradition in the Middle East, and for centuries it was a common practice. It may be coming back. Western influences are creeping in, battling the establishment. Although tattooing is extremely uncommon in Iran, for example, women there are starting to get tattoos that they can display in private, even if they still hide them in public.

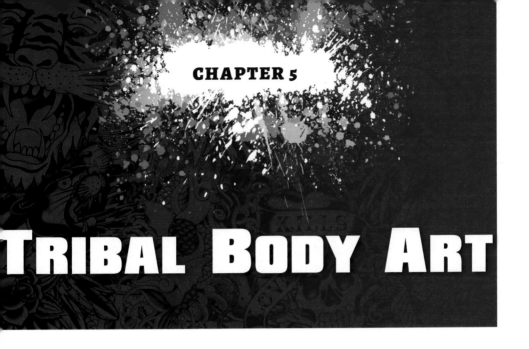

# CHAPTER 5

# TRIBAL BODY ART

Tattooing in tribal cultures is often done as part of tradition. Sometimes it's a mark of a young person's coming of age. Other times, it shows an individual's status within the community. It may even be a recognition of a one's devotion to the gods. Getting a tattoo was a big deal. The pain that the wearer endured, the tattoo's permanence on his body, and the fact that he gave up his life force (blood) to get it, all showed that he was serious.

Tattoos were also believed to have magical powers. People in many cultures got tattoos to protect them against evil spirits or help against sickness. Others used them to help them pass into the afterlife. Both girls and boys were tattooed to show their readiness to be adults in a society. For example, they might show that a boy was able to protect his family and community, and that a girl was up to the task of having children. And, like the right haircut or outfit today, tattoos were considered to make a person more attractive.

## BODY ART OF THE SOUTH PACIFIC TRIBES

The islands of the South Pacific were about warm weather and beachfront living. Native peoples showed lots of skin. Today, the clothes we wear make statements about us. Historically, tribal people used tattoos. To some extent, they still do. Getting a tattoo was not a one-time thing that happened during an impulsive moment. Instead, a person's tattoos were like a collection, with different designs added over the years.

The Kayan, a tribe who lives on the island of Borneo, started tattooing a girl when she turned ten. The process lasted for three or four years, but had to be completed before she gave birth to children. These tattoos often represented a woman's specific abilities—they were like permanent Girl Scout badges. Tattoos also had spiritual significance. People on Borneo thought that without a tattoo, a person would not pass into the spirit world after death. Also, without *enough* tattoos, they might not get the good seats once they got there.

Warriors from the islands of Tonga and Samoa attended ceremonies where they received a tattoo stretching from their lower backs down to their knees. Europeans sometimes called this the trouser tattoo. The designs were an elaborate series of bands and triangles, with some areas completely filled in.

On the Marshall Islands, tattoos reflected the ocean environment. Although the designs were abstract, the marks represented fish, bite marks, and shells. The organization was so detailed and exact that one observer said a fully tattooed man looked like he was "dressed in a suit of chains, resembling a medieval knight."

For centuries, the Maori tribe of New Zealand has practiced an elaborate form of face tattooing called Tā Moko. Symmetrical designs of lines and swirls cover the entire face. Historically, men were more heavily tattooed. Women opted to tattoo their lips and chins, which was considered attractive. The Tā Moko designs had specific elements, but each man's facial design was a little

Members of the Maori tribe practice body art called Tā Moko, a tradition in which the skin is "chiseled" and pigment applied, which leaves permanent markings much like a tattoo.

## JAMES COOK AND THE TAHITIAN "TATAU"

When British explorer James Cook and his crew had been exploring Tahiti and other islands, they were struck by a practice the Tahitians called "tatau." The word meant "to mark." The islanders were tattooed all over their bodies. Cook and his crew didn't know what to make of this strange practice. Joseph Banks was a naturalist on the expedition. He wrote,

> What can be sufficient inducement to suffer so much pain is difficult to say; not one Indian (though I have asked hundreds) would ever give me the least reason for it; possibly superstition may have something to do with it. Nothing else in my opinion could be a sufficient cause for so apparently absurd a custom.

Maybe the men in Cook's crew were a superstitious bunch. After seeing the islanders' tattoos, the sailors wanted them, too. They learned the techniques of tattooing from the natives. Tools made of bone and shell were carved with teeth that were dipped into an oily soot. Then, this comblike instrument was hammered into the skin to transfer the dye.

The boat ride from Tahiti back to England was long. Although they visited the islands in 1769, it was two years before the English sailors landed on their home shore. This gave them plenty of time to practice their new tattooing skills on each other.

The sailors on Cook's voyage brought the art of Polynesian tattoos into modern civilization. New styles of tattoos would develop. New attitudes about them would emerge as it became clear that tattoos were more than skin deep. Getting a tattoo wasn't just an impulsive move. They were a form of art and an expression of culture.

different. His tattoo reflected his status, family heritage, and specific skills. A Maori man knew his tattoo and could draw it to use as his signature.

In 1873, an artist named Gottfried Lindauer visited New Zealand. He painted more than one hundred pictures of Maori men with their tattoos. The collection is now in a museum. It is one of the best historical records of Tā Moko tattoo art.

## IN THE AMERICAS

In South America, the Mayans and Aztecs lived in present-day Mexico and Guatemala. The Incans were farther to the south, in what are now Ecuador, Peru, and Chile. Today, crumbling ruins hint at these great civilizations. But the art that these ancient peoples carved into pottery or built into shrines still lives on in tattoos.

The Aztecs were the dominant culture from the 1300s to the 1500s. Art appreciation started early in the Aztec culture, and arts and crafts were a daily part of life. Their tattoos reflect this. The Aztecs

A common tattoo among the ancient Aztecs was the sun god Huitzilopochtli, shown here. Huitzilopochtli was also a deity of war and human sacrifice.

liked designs that were colorful, detailed, and stylized. Tattoos were received as rites of passage and to show devotion to the gods. The sun god and the warrior god were two common choices. People also got tattoos that reflected the world around them. Animals such as large cats and birds of prey lived in the hostile jungles.

Tattoos served as a kind of identification system. Just as today your student ID card or driver's license says who you are, the color and design of an Aztec tattoo told which tribe a person belonged to.

Also, tattoos often proved a person's worth and status in the tribe. However, there was an exception to this during the Incan period, roughly 1500 BCE to 1500 CE Members of the Incan royalty did not receive tattoos. Their reasoning? The sun god had already made them perfect. A tattoo would spoil that.

Some South American tribes still have an active tradition of tattooing. The Karaja tribe live on an island in central Brazil. Boys and girls here still receive tattoos when they reach puberty. A circle about the size of a penny is tattooed under each eye. Girls sometimes get a blue dot on their chin.

Farther north, in the current countries of the United States and Canada, Native American tribes also got tattoos. Men's tattoos proved their strength, and women's tattoos proclaimed their attractiveness. Today, people of Native American descent often get tattoos to celebrate their heritage.

## A DYING ART FORM?

Tribal tattooing is not nearly as widespread as it once was. In many cultures, the practice has been reduced or abandoned entirely. However, there are some efforts to bring back the old traditions. The old Western ideal—to squash traditional culture in favor of a Christian Euro-pean viewpoint—has lost ground. Instead, there's a new appreciation of the diversity of cultures. As the practice of tattooing becomes more mainstream, the traditional styles are also making a comeback.

Tribal people have also incorporated the imagery of other cultures into their designs. The Iban are a tribe

On the Cook Islands in the central South Pacific, a dancer displays the bold, dark lines of traditional Samoan tattoos.

who live on the coasts in Borneo. They have always adopted tattoos from neighboring tribes and even from outsiders. Traditional designs of dogs and stars are mixed with images that are decidedly modern, like airplanes and helicopters!

Samoan tattooists also incorporated symbols from other cultures. After World War II, for example, the American eagle started appearing in Samoan tattoos.

Some of the original reasons for tattooing are still reflected in today's tattoos. On Tahiti, for example, men like large designs using bold, thick black lines, because the stronger lines are associated with masculinity. Women on Tahiti (not needing to prove their masculinity) generally get only one smaller tattoo.

In 1990, a village on Savai'i, an island in Samoa, made having a tattoo a requirement for men. Today, not only do Samoans living in the islands get traditional tattoos, but so do Samoan immigrants living elsewhere. A tattoo is a way for people to proclaim their heritage and identity even though they have left their native country. The *pe'a* (the traditional body tattoo of Samoa) is becoming popular even with people who are not Samoan. Just as with Captain Cook, tattoos are the ultimate souvenir for tourists. The tourist trade has helped revive traditional tattooing. At the same time, it has also cheapened it, taking away some of its special meaning. This has created a debate in the country: Should non-Samoans get a tattoo that is not traditionally theirs?

Some history has been lost forever. The reasons behind the tattoos, or the circumstances under which they were given, will never be known. However, efforts are being made to revive what traditions do remain.

# GLOSSARY

**ABSTRACT** Not specific, using symbols or designs to represent objects or ideas.

**ANCESTRY** A person's cultural background or heritage.

**CALLIGRAPHY** Lettering that is produced with attention to beauty and form.

**ETHNIC** Related to a specific tribe or culture.

**FANTASTICAL** Not real, existing only in a made-up environment.

**FLASH** Pictures of available tattoo art and designs.

**FLOURISH** To grow and thrive.

**HORIMONO** Traditional Japanese tattoos.

**IMAGERY** Pictures or visual symbols that represent a certain idea.

**PE'A** The traditional body tattoo of Samoans.

**PIGMENT** A coloring or dye.

**PROMINENT** Standing out from surroundings, obvious.

**RITE OF PASSAGE** An event that represents a milestone in human growth or development.

**SACRILEGE** Speaking or acting against God.

**SAK YANT** A type of Buddhist tattoo (also *yantra*).

**SCARIFICATION** The process of scarring the skin to create designs.

**STATUS**  A person's importance or position in society.

**STIGMA**  Something that creates a negative impression.

**SUPERSTITION**  A belief in something, often considered unfounded.

**SYMBOLISM**  Ideas that are represented or implied by images or objects.

**SYMMETRICAL**  The same on both sides; a mirror image.

**TĀ MOKO**  The traditional facial tattooing of the Maori tribe.

**Alliance of Professional Tattooists**
22052 W. 66th Street, Suite 225
Shawnee, KS 66226
(816) 979-1300
Website: www.safe-tattoos.com
The organization, founded in 1992, promotes health
and safety issues related to tattooing.

**American Museum of Natural History**
Central Park West at 79th St.
New York, NY 10024-5192
(212) 769-5100
Website: www.amnh.org
The museum features exhibits on all aspects of natural
history, and has mounted major exhibits on tattooing,
which can be viewed online.

**National Tattoo Association**
485 Business Park Lane
Allentown, PA 18109
(610) 433-7261
Website: www.nationaltattooassociation.com
Founded in 1976, this organization strives to promote
the idea of tattooing as art to the general public, as
well as ensure safety and quality within the industry.

**Tattoo Archive**
618 West 4th St.
Winston-Salem, NC 27101
(336) 722-4422
Website: http://www.tattooarchive.com
Operated through the Tattoo Archive store, PRTRC
 works with tattoo artists and enthusiasts to preserve
 and document tattoo history.

**Thomas Lockhart's West Coast Tattoo Museum**
2108 East Hastings Street
Vancouver, BC
Canada V5L 1V1
(604) 681-2049
Website: http://www.westcoasttattoo.com/tattoo
 _museum.htm
In his Vancouver studio, tattoo artist Thomas Lockhart displays unusual tattooing artifacts from
 around the world.

**Triangle Tattoo & Museum**
356 B North Main Street
Fort Bragg, CA 95437
(707) 964-8814
Website: http://www.triangletattoo.com

Founded in 1986, the museum displays tattoo artifacts from around the world and curates exhibits on
different styles and trends in tattoo art.

**University of Pennsylvania Museum of Archaeology
and Anthropology**
"Bodies of Cultures: A World Tour of Body Modification"
3260 South Street
Philadelphia, PA 19104
(215) 898-4000
Website: https://www.penn.museum/sites/body
_modification/bodmodintro.shtml
Founded in 1887, the Penn Museum is the largest university museum in the United States and one of the world's
great archeology and anthropology research museums.
This website provides a guided tour through the objects
in its collection related to body art.

Ashcraft, Brian, and Hori Benny. *Japanese Tattoos: History, Culture, Design*. North Clarendon, Vermont: Tuttle Publishing, 2016.

Cohen, Robert. *Body Piercing and Tattooing*. New York, NY: Rosen Publishing, 2013.

Friedman, Anna F. *The World Atlas of Tattoo*. New Haven, CT: Yale University Press, 2015.

Johansson, Andreas. *Yakuza Tattoo*. Årsta, Sweden: Dokument Press, 2017.

Mccomb, David. *100 Years of Tattoos*. London, England: Laurence King Publishing, 2015.

Mcewan, Emily. *The Scottish Gaelic Tattoo Handbook: Authentic Words and Phrases in the Celtic Language of Scotland*. Halifax, Nova Scotia: Bradan Press, 2016.

Mifflin, Margot. *Bodies of Subversion: A Secret History of Women and Tattoo*. New York, NY: Powerhouse Books, 2013.

Quarto Publishing. *Body Piercing: The Body Art Manual*. Minneapolis, MN: Quarto Publishing Group, 2010.

Pierrat, Jerome, and Alfred. *The Little Book of Knowledge: Tattoos*. San Diego, CA: IIDW Publishing, 2017.

Smith, Trent, and Ashley Tyson. *The Tattoo Dictionary: An A–Z Guide to Choosing Your Tattoo*. London, England: Mitchell Beazley, 2016.

Watkins, Jack. *Tattoo: Symbols And Meanings*. New York, NY: Chartwell Books, 2016.

# BIBLIOGRAPHY

Asiantattoonline.com. "Asia tattoo history and modern fact." June 2, 2010. http://www.asiantattooonline.com/2010/06/02/tattoo-history-and-modern-actual-fact-in-asia.

Bjorkell, Stina. "Skin deep: the art of tattooing in China." Radio86.co.uk. November 28, 2007. http://www.radio86.co.uk/explore-learn/lifestyle-in-china/4562/skin-deep-the-art-of-tattooing-in-china.

Corney, John. "The Picts, the tattooed aboriginal tribes of Scotland." Ariki Art. Retrieved August 8, 2010. http://www.arikiart.com/tattoo-body-art/tribal-tattoos.htm.

DeMello, Margo. *Bodies of Inscription: A Cultural History of the Modern Tattoo Community*. Durham, NC: Duke University Press, 2000.

Finan, Eileen. "Is art just skin deep?" *Time*, April 22, 2002. http://www.time.com/time/magazine/article/0,9171,901020429-232672,00.html.

Gilbert, Steve. *Tattoo History: A Source Book*. New York, NY: Juno Books, 2000.

Helfrich, Benjamin. "The needle for the nail: Christians showing faith, independence through tattoo." News21. Retrieved August 8, 2010. http://newsinitiative.org/story/2007/08/16/christian_tattoo_the_needle_for.

Ho, Gary, with Jeremy Hogan, Meghan Hoke, Nathan Holmes, Mariko Ikemori, Michael Jordan and Joby

Joy. "History of tattoos around the world." Retrieved August 16, 2010. http://www.spaceports.com /~meggie/psu/art002/tattoos.

Krcmarik, Katherine L. "Tattooing around the world." Retrieved August 16, 2010. https://www.msu .edu/~krcmari1/individual/world.html.

Lineberry, Cate. "Tattoos: the ancient and mysterious history." Smithsonian.com, January 1, 2007. http:// www.smithsonianmag.com/history-archaeology /tattoo.html.

Miller, Jean-Chris. *The Body Art Book*. New York, NY: Berkley Publishing Group, 2004.

NationalGeographic.com. "Tattoos." Retrieved August 8, 2010. http://www.nationalgeographic.com/tattoos.

Ong, Tan. "Buddhist Tattoos: A New Trend in Singapore." *The Chakra*, February 17, 2010. http://www .chakranews.com/buddhist-tattoos-a-new-trend-in -singapore/261.

Paquette, David. "Tattoo not taboo." *The Irrawaddy*, February 2008. http://www.irrawaddy.org/article .php?art_id=10096&page=1.

PBS.org. "Skin stories: the art and culture of Polynesian tattoo." Retrieved August 8, 2010. http://www .pbs.org/skinstories/culture/index.html.

Polhemus, Ted. *Hot Bodies, Cool Styles: New Techniques in Self-Adornment*. New York, NY: Thames & Hudson, Inc., 2004.

Rio, Dale, and Eva Banchini. *Tattoo*. Philadelphia, PA: Running Press Book Publishers, 2004.

"Tattoo Museum." Retrieved August 14, 2010. http://www.vanishingtattoo.com/tattoo_museum/index.html.

Thomas, Nicholas, with Anna Cole and Bronwen Douglas, eds. *Tattoo: Bodies, Art, and Exchange in the Pacific and the West*. Durham, NC: Duke University Press, 2005.

Van Dinter, Maarten Hesselt. *The World of Tattoo: An Illustrated History*. Amsterdam, The Netherlands: KIT Publishers, 2005.

Yoon, Cindy. "The history of the tattoo." Asia Society, May 28, 2003. http://asiasociety.org/style-living /popular-culture/the-history-tattoo.

Young, M. *Agony and Alchemy*. Prescott, AZ: Hohm Press, 2005.

# INDEX

## ABOUT THE AUTHORS

Nicholas Faulkner is a writer living in New Jersey.

Diane Bailey has written multiple books for children and young adults on subjects ranging from sports to states to celebrities. While researching and writing this book, she was fascinated with how this traditional art form has become the ultimate in contemporary culture. Bailey lives in Kansas with her two teenage sons.

## PHOTO CREDITS